THE MISTRESS CALLED MINISTRY

Apostle Melvin Thompson III

THE MISTRESS CALLED MINISTRY

Helping God's Leaders

Outskirts Press, Inc.
Denver, Colorado

TABLE OF CONTENTS

ACKNOWLEDGMENTS

I would like to thank Prophetess Tashya Thompson, my wife. Thank you so much for being my greatest supporter and encourager and for understanding the time I needed to spend alone with God. I would like to thank my former spiritual father, Pastor Hubert Hall, who went on to be with the Lord, for his many years of impartation into my life -- there are really no words to express my appreciation for the many deposits he released into my life. I would like to thank God for Melvin Thompson IV, my son, for his time in letting Daddy go to work on this book and when I am called away for ministry. I would like thank God for my dad, Pastor Melvin Thompson, for his many years of encouragement, and to my mother, Kathi Blanding, for allowing me to be you're Apostle; I count it an honor to be able to serve my mother in the kingdom of God. I would like to thank all of my spiritual sons and daughters in the kingdom of God who have prayed for me and my wife to deliver the books that God has birthed in our hearts. Last but not least to my All Nations Church family that continues to be a great blessing to me and my wife, and to our presbytery, who holds up the apostolic and prophetic vision of our local assembly.

INTRODUCTION

I would like to begin this book by letting you know how it came about. In March of 2010, the Lord began to put a prophetic burden on my heart for the situations that I started to see unfolding in kingdom marriages all over the world. I began to see that many kingdom leaders have a false balance as it relates to the work of ministry, and I watched many leaders become overly engaged in the work of ministry, but at the same time put little time into building their marriages and children in the things of God. When we look at this, we see how many marriages and families have been destroyed in the name of ministry. But as an apostolic voice to this generation, I'm called and sent by God to declare balance back to the leadership in the Body of Christ. So as we take our journey into this book, you will find that even though it is titled *The Mistress Called Ministry*, it is not limited to male leadership having an affair with ministry, but this book will speak both to men and women of God who have become more in love with the work of ministry than with their husbands and wives. This is not a book to discourage you from enjoying what God has called you to do, but a book that will challenge you to maintain balance in whatever you do in the kingdom of God.

We can all agree that we have seen men and women of God have great schedules -- some of them are gone 200 days out of a year and they are busy building ministry, but are failing to minister to their marriages that are falling apart. As I sat back and watched the many kingdom marriages that have really been destroyed by the lack of balance, it dawned on me that leaders have become more excited about preaching crusades, doing revivals, and traveling the world than they are in keeping their love relationship with their spouse in check. There are many women who are wounded because they feel that their husbands are having an affair with a mistress called ministry. Many of them go to church out of duty but in their heart they are holding so much hurt -- the reason why they are hurt is because their husbands spend more time talking on the phone to others, preaching at different conferences, staying at the church, and doing many other things that revolve around ministry, but then they deprive their wives of valuable time with them. Then you have on the other hand men of God who are hurt because they look and see their wives in the spotlight of ministry, where many people respect them and call them spiritual mothers, but their husbands are discouraged because they do not see their wives perform motherly duties to their natural children.

So you have both men and women of God who feel like their spouses are more in love with ministry than they are with them. We have seen an all-out attack in the Body of Christ against kingdom marriages, which is designed by the enemy to make it look like the gospel that we preach is not able to keep our marriages together. This is not to offend any men or women of God who have been through a terrible divorce, but its purpose is to stop the plan of the enemy right now from destroying more marriages in the kingdom because of false balance. Let's look into the word of God to help us understand how God feels about false balance in the lives of leaders and believers.

Proverbs 11:1

A false balance is abomination to the Lord: But a just weight is his delight.

As we see in the scripture above, God says that a false balance is abomination to him -- therefore when we walk in false balance, we are coming short of the glory of God. I will be the first to let you know that when it comes to balance, I failed at it in the first year of my marriage. I can remember when God started to deal with me about investing more in my wife than I was into everyone else. He showed me in several different ways. The first way He showed me was through an experience I had with some former members of our church. Here is what happened: I had spent time pouring into these believers and really imparting Godly wisdom into their lives, week after week, staying at the church after service, not coming straight home, really giving them a lot of time because I wanted to build them so they could help build the ministry. But there came a day when I had to bring strong correction to them -- and what happened was that they got upset and left the church. It was then that the Holy Spirit showed me when you have given your all to people and sometimes you get disappointed, which is apart of the course, your wife is still there loving you, praying for you, and supporting you.

Some of you may be asking, "What are you saying, then? Are you saying don't invest in people?" No, I'm not saying don't invest in people -- but what I'm saying is don't put the work of ministry before your spouse. The second way that God dealt with me about this was He said to me, "Son, you made the choice to marry this woman of God and you are responsible to make sure that before you lead my people into great places of my Spirit, that you lead her first." So I say today that because of the grace of God I have learned to have balance in my life so that I don't apostolically upgrade the world and leave my wife in the same place. I would like to give prophetic declaration to those who are reading this book: I declare by the time that you get done reading this book, your marriage will be restored, your family will be healed, and balance will become an important part of your life.

So now as you go further into the pages of this book, I have a confession I would like to make to you -- I'm no longer in an affair with the mistress who was called ministry. But now I love God first, family second, and the work of ministry is third -- and guess what? Ministry is no longer a mistress that I spend more time with, because my wife and I enjoy changing cities, shaking regions, and taking nations together, and I declare I will never again let ministry have my wife's position in my life.

What Is a Mistress?

Webster's dictionary defines the word <u>mistress</u> as "a woman who has ultimate control over something (the mistress of our affection)." The Merriam-Webster dictionary defines a mistress this way: "A woman other than his wife whom a married man has a continuing intimate relationship with." A mistress is a man's long-term female lover and companion who is not married to him, especially used when the man is married to another woman. The relationship generally is stable and at least semi-permanent; however, the couple does not live together openly. Also the relationship is usually but not always secret, and there is the implication that a mistress may be kept.

As we see here, there are many different definitions of what the world considers a mistress to be. But I would really like to focus on the first definition, which lets us know that the mistress gains control of one's affections. This is powerful in that it shows us how many leaders allow ministry to become the center of their affection. Then what happens is that they show more respect, encouragement, and attention to the mistress called ministry. They show passion to the work of ministry and they disrespect their wife or husband. So when they get angry, they make statements such as "Whether you are here or not, I'm going to do ministry." It is also stated that "All I need is ministry, and not you." These types of statements make the spouse feel unwanted. Many times when they are in an affair with ministry, they think that it will be permanent; also the affair with ministry is usually kept quiet and secret. Many times they will get up and say how great God is moving in the ministry, but never share with the people how God is working with their marriage. The reason for this is that many of them think that they are pleasing God by working for Him while they are overlooking the needs of their spouse and are family. We have many in the Body of Christ who are in an affair with ministry, but many of them won't confess this, because they feel it is all right to be like that. Why is this so wrong in the sight of God? Let's look into scripture to find out.

Ephesians 5:24-26 (King James Version)

[24]Therefore as the church is subject unto Christ, so let the wives be to their own husbands in every thing.

[25]Husbands, love your wives, even as Christ also loved the church, and gave himself for it;

[26]That he might sanctify and cleanse it with the washing of water by the word,

Based upon this scripture we can see why it is wrong to have an affair with ministry. The Bible instructs wives to be subject to their own husbands as the church is subject to Christ. If this be the case, then we must deal with the women of God first. The scripture did not say to the wives to be subject unto the work of ministry, and then to your husband -- it said to be subject to your own husband. I would like to say here when it says "own husband" in this passage, its really telling you not to be spending more time in the work of ministry with other people's husbands and not spending enough time with your own husband. I also know that there may be some theologians reading this book who may feel that I'm not explaining the text in context. But what I'm doing is releasing revelation through the scripture that goes far beyond human intellect, so that people can see the danger of misplaced priorities. As we move on, we understand that husbands should love their wives even as Christ also loved the church. Now this is a big statement made by the Apostle Paul, because he did not say "Love the work of ministry as Christ loved the church." He said "Love your wife as Christ loves the church." Well the question would have to be asked: "How much did Christ love the church?" The gospel according to John will help us to see how much He really loved the church.

John 15:13 (King James Version)

[13]Greater love hath no man than this, that a man lay down his life for his friends.

According to this scripture, we will see that Christ loved the church so much that He was willing to lay down his life. Those of you who are reading this book don't need me to go into who the church is. Those of you who understand you're the church also understand that Christ laid down His life so that you can have freedom. Looking at this scripture it would be safe to say that husbands should love their wives the same way Christ loved the church. Just like Jesus gave himself for the church, so then every husband needs to give himself for his wife. Therefore, you cannot love your wife even as Christ loved the church if you are giving yourself more to the work of ministry than to your spouse. Many men are running around the world preaching, and their wives are depressed, discouraged, and down. I say to every man of God who is out there reaching out to other men's wives while your wife is at home broken, get home and minister to your wife.

Many times we in the Body of Christ say that men and women of God are anointed because of the miracles, signs, and wonders we see God using them to perform. But when you mature, you look at things differently, because you say if they are anointed to reach every one else, then what is the problem with them being able to reach their own spouse? As I was studying and researching in the midst of writing this book, I came across a true and powerful testimony of a pastor that will help bring even more clarity to what I'm saying. Every fivefold ministry gift I would like you to read the next portion of this book with an open heart. I will change the names in the article for the sake of confidentiality. So we will call the man Pastor Joseph, and his wife we will call Elizabeth.

Pastor Joseph's True Story

I had anticipated this moment with an emotional mixture of intimidation and challenge. The intimidation was generated by the fact that I was standing before a large group of my fellow pastors and I was to deliver the opening address at our annual Pastors' Conference. The element of challenge found its focus in the question, "How can I outflank their professional communication skills and their ability to anticipate what they think I'm about to say? How can I arrest their attention long enough to make my point?"

I decided to take a risk and begin with a confession that would need more than a little explanation!

"I begin tonight with a very difficult confession before you, my fellow pastors. There is no simple or easy way to say this; so I will just say it: I have been guilty of having an affair."

The tension level took a quantum leap upward! Some of those sitting in front of me were my peers. I had trained with these men for ministry. I noted some looks of stunned disbelief. Others showed their disbelief in smiles that indicated that they knew I had to have an angle here of some kind!

I continued: "In one sense, I can think of no better place to make such a confession than in the presence of other pastors, because most of you will have long since recognized your own vulnerability. In another sense, I can think of no worse place to acknowledge my failure because the judgment of my peers has the potential to be the worst kind of condemnation.

"Now I can almost hear you ask the question, 'How can one who is supposedly committed to the Lord Jesus and to his own wife ever allow another relationship to develop to the point where those two holy relationships are endangered?'

"As best I can determine, it began with a flaw or weakness in my own character that was (and is) wide open to exploitation. Like many of you, I have a need to be needed and to be affirmed. Sometimes I think that need is above and beyond what might be considered healthy. I further acknowledge that I am at my most vulnerable when there is an absence of encouragement and affirmation in my emotional diet."

Well, so far my explanation was not doing very much to lessen the tension level. I pressed on....

"My mistress was very subtle. She knew my emotional need for praise and affirmation in my life, and she was quick to meet that need. Time and again she was ready to speak warmly of my qualities as a person and my endeavors as a pastor. In return, she seemed to require so little -- initially, at least. She repeatedly assured me that our developing relationship need not negatively affect my relationship with Elizabeth, my wife, or with the Lord.

At first she had told me she would be satisfied if I offered her only the time that was left after my prior relational responsibilities. It seemed that I could have my cake and eat it, too! It all seemed so legitimate...so rational...so inviting...so fulfilling...just too good to be true!

"But as time passed, this seemingly free liaison became increasingly demanding. I began to realize that I was becoming both enmeshed in and addicted to the relationship.

"My mistress was demanding more and more of my time. She began to begrudge the time I gave to Elizabeth and my family. She also began to make demands on the time I had initially reserved for the Lord."

At this point, I became aware that a number of my listeners were becoming restless in their chairs while others sat like statues as though any movement might betray an inner response of guilt. I was beginning to wonder if my approach was a bad choice. Too late now, so I continued:

"As I tried to meet those demands, the intensity of my guilt began to increase. My priority commitments to my Lord and my wife came under enormous pressure. I found myself making excuses for the decreasing amount of time I was spending with Elizabeth. I kept telling her that my lack of time with her and the family was part of the sacrifice we had to make for the sake of the Lord's work. I seemed to be forever asking forgiveness from God because of what I was allowing to happen in my relationship with Him.

"Another complicating and destructive factor in all this mess was that my mistress was now claiming that she, too, had needs that only I could meet. I found myself in the terrible situation of becoming indispensable to her, and that just added to the feelings of fragmentation. The whole dynamic had become like a spiritual 'Fatal Attraction.' It sounds stupid even as I say it but, as demanding as she became, even that price was worth paying when I lost sight of where my needs were supposed to be met and tried to meet them with her. The paradox is that I have both warmly welcomed her and deeply resented her. I have sought consolation with her, and yet I have despised the cost of that comfort."

I now began to note some further changes in the facial expressions of my listeners. Some, at least, were beginning to suspect that this was not what it first appeared to be! Some mental gears were beginning to turn in another direction as they tried to pre-empt just where I was going with this "confession." It seems that even pastors don't want to be the last to get it!

"I began by confessing to you that I had a mistress. I deliberately made that statement in the past tense. I did so partly as a statement of fact and partly as a statement of hope. It is a statement of fact inasmuch as, at this point in time, I do not have a mistress. That destructive relationship is now broken and is part of my history. I have owned it and I have been forgiven.

"It is a statement of hope inasmuch as I fully realize that I am capable of re-commencing that liaison at any time, particularly during those periods of emotional weakness when others seem insensitive to my needs. I know that she is always there, ready to meet that need.

"And now, as part of my confession, I have determined to complete my confessional atonement before you by actually naming my mistress to you."

The tension that had started to ease with some was quickly restored with this last remark! In fact, I was to find out later that two or three had determined by this time to get out of their seats and leave the room.

"I name her in your presence because, as I have listened to fellow pastors talk over the years, I believe some of you also know her and you may want to join me in my confession and atonement.

"Her name is 'MINISTRY'."

The tension level, which had varied quite noticeably to this point, now relaxed very noticeably!

"Ah, yes! I can see from the looks on some faces that there are those of you who are acquainted with her. That being the case, perhaps you might like to journey with me a little further as I try to explain the process of recovery and restoration to my wife and to my God that has happened for me.

"Before I ask you to walk further with me in this exposé, I need first to make another confession and, perhaps, an apology.

"I recognize that, in using the analogy of an affair to make a point, I have run the very serious risk of piercing the hearts of those who may be struggling with a more literal affair or relationship than what I have described. If I have unwittingly and unhelpfully wounded you, I do ask for your forgiveness and understanding. On the other hand, if my analogy has pierced your heart with conviction, I do not apologize for that.

"The reason I have been prepared to take the risk in describing the dynamics of this unhealthy relationship with 'ministry' in terms of an affair is that I really believe that 'ministry' can become a destructive 'affair of the heart' with the capacity to estrange us from our families. I, for one, have felt times of enormous pressure and conflict of interest as I have sought to be both a loving husband and a faithful pastor. In retrospect, I can see that those pressures have been largely of my own making, and have emerged in my life because of my failure to understand the true relationship that I was to have with 'ministry.'

"Let me explain first how the Lord Jesus moved to expose and correct what had become an idol in my life. Even now it sounds strange to refer to 'ministry' as an idol. But if an idol is something to which one devotes the major portion of one's time, energy, and effort...if an idol is that for which I am willing to sacrifice just about everything in my life...if an idol is anything that comes between me and my God and competes for that devotion, loyalty, and commitment that ought to belong only to Him...then 'ministry' had become such an idol...such a mistress.

"As I think back now, one of the factors that led to the emergence of this form of idolatry was the confusion that developed when I lost sight of the fact that God had called me to Himself before ever He called me to 'the ministry.'

"I have been challenged again by the call of the early disciples recorded in Mark 3 where the purpose for which Jesus called His disciples was '..that they might be with Him and that He might send them out to preach...'

"That sequence has now become so important to me. God has called us first of all to Himself. He first says, 'Come to me...' before He says, 'Go into all the world...' All ministry must flow out of that reality. Of course, if you had asked me at any point in my thirty years of pastoral ministry if I believed that, truthfully I would have answered with a prompt 'Yes!' But that answer would have come from my head, not my heart. The truth is that there is a lot I affirm with my head which, if my actions are any indication, I do not really believe in my heart.

"There is a key passage in Luke 10 that has helped me regain a perspective that my former mistress took from me. When the seventy-two disciples returned from their ministry assignment, they were ecstatic that even the demons were subject to the authority that Christ had given them. They had experienced a good time with 'ministry'! I hear in their words feelings of fulfillment, excitement, and anticipation for what the future might hold by way of further ministry.

"However, Jesus firmly added a corrective to their understandable enthusiasm. He said to them: 'I have given you authority to overcome all the power of the enemy. However, do not rejoice that the spirits submit to you, but rejoice that your names are written in heaven.' (Luke 10:20)

Jesus was identifying for them -- and for us -- the only source and basis of joy and rejoicing, and it was not in the 'ministry.' Sure, we may be grateful for those times of blessing that result from what we do for Him, but the only appropriate, unchanging, and dependable source of joy is in our relationship with Jesus... in the fact that our names are written down in heaven and we are secure in that fact!

"Like some of you, I have often made the mistake of finding my joy elsewhere...especially with 'ministry'...and she has a way of becoming a mistress...an idol. Too often my perspective and mood swings are directly affected by 'ministry'! My source of joy becomes confused and I find myself on an emotional roller-coaster. I have also discovered that it is so easy, as a pastor, to develop a 'professional' relationship with Jesus. In that kind of relationship, He is the 'employer' and I am the 'employee.'

"By contrast, I was challenged by the basis of Jesus' joy identified in the same passage: 'At that time, Jesus, full of joy through the Holy Spirit said, "I praise you, Father, Lord of heaven and earth...Yes, Father, for this was your good pleasure."' (Luke 10:21). Here is the heartbeat of Jesus in terms of His relationship with His Father. His source of joy was in the other two members of the Godhead -- the Father and the Holy Spirit.

"Maybe that is why we never see Jesus centered upon the results of His ministry as though that was the beginning and end of everything. He never allowed 'ministry' to become His mistress. He knew how to say 'No' without feeling guilty. He knew how and when to serve, and how and when to retreat...even in the midst of the demands and expectations of those about Him. Luke records these simple but telling words in chapter 5:16: 'The news about Him spread all the more so that crowds of people came to hear him and be healed of their sicknesses. But Jesus often withdrew to lonely places and prayed.'

"Prayer retreats in the midst of human need! What kind of pastor is this?

"I hear echoes of that same demanding insistence in the words of the disciples when Jesus had gone out early in the morning to pray. In Mark 1:37, we are told that they came to Him and said, 'Everyone is looking for you!' Roughly translated, that seems to me to mean, 'You are indispensable! They can't do without you! Prayer is nice in its right place but you don't have time for that luxury right now! We are surrounded by need!'

"Jesus' response is both startling and instructive: 'Let us go somewhere else -- to the nearby villages -- so I can preach there also. That is why I have come.' (Mark 1:38)

"What kind of pastor indeed! The answer is simple and disturbing. Jesus was a shepherd/pastor who knew what His Father wanted Him to do and He did it -- nothing more, nothing less, and nothing else. He was the kind of pastor who, at the end of His earthly ministry, could say, 'I have completed the work that you gave me to do'! (John 17:4). He fulfilled God's agenda for Him, not the expectations of countless other people. He was the kind of pastor who found his joy in His relationship with God, not in what He did for God!

"While I am grateful for what God does through 'ministry,' I am nowhere called to rejoice in the ministry or to rejoice in who I am or what I am doing. I am to be with Jesus and to rejoice in Him and in the relationship He has established with me as expressed in the fact that my name is written in heaven.

"Part of my restoration process has been to set aside every Wednesday afternoon for a personal retreat time when I go away from my office and my home and I spend time with Jesus -- not Jesus my employer, but Jesus, the lover of my soul. That's our time. I try not to talk 'business' with Him in that setting…if you understand what I mean.

"Knowing my own initial response to God's call for that time to be set aside, I am fairly certain that there are those of you who are now assuring yourselves that there is no way you can afford to be so extravagant with your use of time. In your priorities, such time allocation, while perhaps desirable, is not possible. You are busy telling yourself that the demands on your time are such that they exclude any possibility of three or four hours spent with the Lord in a block like that each week. Brothers and sisters, those words are being seductively whispered in your heart by the mistress... 'ministry.' I know because she has seduced me time and again with the same rationale. There is so much to be done, isn't there?

"All that brings me to another Biblical address that I have often had to visit. It is again in Luke 10. This time it is the domestic scene recorded in verses 38-42.

"The Lord has repeatedly drawn my attention to the difference between Martha and Mary...Martha, the activist, and Mary, the listener. The question with which God has often challenged me is, 'Who most clearly reflects your priorities -- Martha or Mary?'

"The answer is usually Martha. Now, you and I are hardly in a position to question her heart and her motives. They may well have been of the highest caliber. But what we are told is what was happening to her on the inside as she gave herself to 'ministry.' The three words used of her emotional condition are 'distracted,' 'worried,' and 'upset.'

"Please don't get me wrong here. Someone had to prepare the meal. Someone had to be out in the kitchen. But the challenge to me is what was happening to Martha in terms of her attitude. Did you pick up on the resentment that was fermenting toward her sister? The water on the stove wasn't the only thing boiling out in the kitchen that day! 'Lord, don't you care that my sister has left me to do the work by myself? Tell her to help me!' (Luke 10:40)

"She was becoming resentful toward her sister and dictatorial toward her Lord! She presumed to direct Jesus as to what He should do to get her immobile sister mobile! How often I have done that over the years! Jesus was again gracious but firm in His evaluation of the condition of Martha's heart.

"He corrected Martha and commended Mary. Martha was committed to the urgent, whereas Mary was committed to the important. Martha opened her home, whereas Mary opened her heart. Martha gave her service, whereas Mary gave herself.

"I don't think it is coincidental that I hear in that exchange an echo of what God has often said to my heart. Have you not had times when, in your genuine desire to serve the Lord, you have become distracted by all the things that had to be done? You have become worried and upset over the many things. You have become resentful toward your brothers and sisters in Christ because they seem to have been immobile when they should have been up and working. You have become resentful and guilty about the time your wife and family seemed to expect.

"You have even presumed to complain to the Lord of the Church in such a way as to suggest that, if He paid some attention to your plight, He might just begin to do things the way you think they should be done. When those dynamics begin to emerge, we can be sure that 'ministry' has successfully seduced us and become our mistress.

"But what about that other prior relationship in all this... my relationship with my wife, Elizabeth? We have just celebrated our wedding anniversary. We have three great kids, two delightful daughters-in-law and five wonderful granddaughters!! As I look back over the almost forty years that I have been a pastor, I can say that my wife has been very understanding about many, many aspects of what it means for me to be a pastor and her place as my wife.

"She has been less than understanding about my mistress!

"I recall how, when we were in our sixth year of pastoral ministry back in the early seventies, Elizabeth first tried to speak to me about how 'ministry' was coming between us. I couldn't understand why she felt as she did because, after all, we were doing the Lord's work! From time to time she tried to explain how she felt and why, but it was to no avail. I was blind to the fact that the dynamics of the 'eternal triangle' were appearing in our relationship. Only it was due to not another woman. But it was a mistress, sure enough.

"Elizabeth was teaching school at the time and, because I had relatively little time for her, she began to apply herself in her work to the point where, on one day of rare enlightenment for me, I found myself thinking that she seemed to care more for her work than she did for me!

"And suddenly my eyes were opened! Within twenty-four hours of that revelation, I was down at the travel agent trying to organize a holiday just for the two of us. It proved to be a smart move! We had a great time away together and a new start in our relationship when we came home.

"You would think that I would have learned from that experience, wouldn't you? The truth is that my mistress was waiting to seduce me as soon as we came back. I have had to learn that the commitment of giving my wife the priority she deserves as my God-given partner in life is never static. It is always dynamic, in the sense that it is a daily choice.

"Over the years since that first realization, I have sought to give to Elizabeth the time commitment she deserves as my wife, but it has been with varying degrees of success and failure.

"From time to time, she has suggested that I should take time out from pastoral ministry so that we could have extended time as a family without those unique demands and expectations that constitute pastoral ministry. The very idea was anathema! Didn't she realize I was needed... even indispensable?!

"Somehow I had become so involved again with my mistress that to even think of extended leave was tantamount to a betrayal of some kind! I look back now and I can see that what Elizabeth was suggesting, in effect, was a sabbatical: a God-ordained principle…a period of refreshment and renewal of our spiritual and emotional lives and our relationship together.

"It was still some time before I began realizing something else that was obvious to Elizabeth long before it dawned on me. I was losing my cutting edge. The vision of the Lord and a right understanding of my relationship to ministry had again become fuzzy. I was getting tired in the ministry…not physically tired, but emotionally and spiritually weary. Although I took holidays and long service leave, the benefits seemed very short-lived.

"It was toward the end of the 1980s that these realizations began to dawn and I can recall sharing with the church leadership what Elizabeth had been saying for quite some time: namely, a growing sense that I was finding little fulfillment and a lot of tiredness and that I needed to take extended leave. So clearly did the Lord seem to say, "Come with me by yourselves to a quiet place and get some rest". (Mark 6:31)

"I feel free of the mistress at the moment, but I know that I need to daily monitor her attempts to seduce me and my response to her. I have come to accept that I will live with this tension for the rest of my pastoral life. It will involve daily choices for me. Somehow, I feel at peace about that prospect now that the 'enemy' has been identified and her tactics are out in the open. I am also encouraged by the fact that the antidote to her poison has also been identified: a daily yielding of my life to my Lord and to my wife.

"NOW YOU CAN ANSWER -- IS MINISTRY YOUR MISTRESS?

Is Ministry a Mistress?

As we closed the previous chapter of this book, I know many of you have questions about the work of ministry. Some of you by now think that I am calling ministry itself a mistress. Then there are some of you who think I'm painting a bad picture of ministry. My purpose is not to do any of that, but to show you how ministry, when not placed in the right position in your life, can become a mistress. In this chapter I'm going to bring clarity to what the Spirit of God is showing us through this book.

Ephesians 4:12 (King James Version)

[12]For the perfecting of the saints, for the work of the ministry, for the edifying of the body of Christ...

We can see from this scripture above, which was written by the

Apostle Paul, that God has given unto us fivefold ministry gifts for the perfecting of the saints. So we can say that without the work of ministry we would not be perfected; therefore the ministry that God has given is necessary for us to be able to move into the deeper things of God. So let's define what ministry is. Ministry is defined as the service, function, and or profession of a minister. So this shows us that ministry is serving as sons and daughters in the Kingdom of God, and functioning in what God has placed upon our life. Then we are able to say that ministry is God's will for the people of God. So we understand that ministry is supposed to be something that we enjoy doing because it is a part of obeying God. If ministry in its purest form is not a mistress, then how does ministry become a mistress? Ministry becomes a mistress when it is taken outside the God-ordained boundaries. When you are married, there are boundaries that come with you performing the work of ministry. I'm not saying that you can't do ministry, but what I'm telling you is that you can't do ministry at the expense of losing your family. Ministry is from God to impact the lives of people everywhere. I would like to show you how Adam failed his wife, in the book of Genesis.

Genesis 2:15 (King James Version)

[15]And the LORD God took the man, and put him into the garden of Eden to dress it and to keep it.

Now we see that in the beginning God gave Adam specific instructions when He put him in the garden. God told Adam to dress the garden, which means to work in it and enjoy it. Then he told him to keep it. The Hebrew word for keep is *shamar,* and it means to guard, to keep, and to be a watchman. You must understand what the word "guard" means so that you can fully understand the word "keep," because they are intertwined. To guard means to protect, watch over, stand guard over, police, secure, defend, shield, shelter, screen, cover, cloak, preserve, save, conserve, supervise, keep under surveillance, control, keep under guard, govern, restrain, suppress, keep watch, be alert, take care. Then there are synonyms for the noun "guard," which are protector, defender guardian, custodian, watchman, sentinel, sentry, patrol, and garrison. So as we understand the definition of keep, we see that this was a great responsibility given to Adam. Now I know when we begin to talk about this story, there are a lot of different opinions in the Body of Christ, but here I would like just to release a thought that will provoke you to study a little deeper than what you have considered in this Scripture. Let's look at Genesis 3:1-7.

Genesis 3:1-7 (King James Version)

¹Now the serpent was more subtil than any beast of the field which the LORD God had made. And he said unto the woman, Yea, hath God said, Ye shall not eat of every tree of the garden?

²And the woman said unto the serpent, We may eat of the fruit of the trees of the garden:

³But of the fruit of the tree which is in the midst of the garden, God hath said, Ye shall not eat of it, neither shall ye touch it, lest ye die.

[4]And the serpent said unto the woman, Ye shall not surely die:

[5]For God doth know that in the day ye eat thereof, then your eyes shall be opened, and ye shall be as gods, knowing good and evil.

[6]And when the woman saw that the tree was good for food, and that it was pleasant to the eyes, and a tree to be desired to make one wise, she took of the fruit thereof, and did eat, and gave also unto her husband with her; and he did eat.

[7]And the eyes of them both were opened, and they knew that they were naked; and they sewed fig leaves together, and made themselves aprons.

Here in this third chapter of Genesis, we begin to see how the enemy beguiled Eve. But I have a question for you who are reading this book: Where was Adam when a serpent was talking to his wife? Remember God gave him the mandate to watch over the garden, so what was he doing while the serpent was talking to his wife? Could it be that Adam was too busy dressing -- which means working and enjoying the garden -- so that he was not fulfilling the responsibility that God gave him to protect, watch over, stand guard against, govern, defend, and shield and all of the other things that define "keep"? The second thing we need to ask ourselves is whether the serpent talks to Adam before he deceived his wife? Our answer from a scriptural point of view would be no, because the Bible never shows us where Adam talked to a serpent. If this be the case, then why would Adam let a serpent who never talked to him when he was alone, start talking to his wife now that he was married? I understand many people have a traditional view regarding this scripture. Many have a view that it was really all Eve's fault, and the reason you may have this view is because you grew up in a denomination that has issues with women; therefore they find every scripture in the Bible to accuse, oppress, and bind women.

The next thing we see is that somehow or another Adam had to let Eve know that they were not allowed to eat from the fruit of the tree which was in the midst of the garden. But the thing that has me puzzled again is where in the world is Adam WHILE HIS WIFE IS TALKING TO A SERPENT FOR THIS LONG? After all of this, we see that the serpent was able to deceive Eve. I believe the serpent was able to take advantage of Eve because Adam was not watching like he was supposed to. I pray that now you can see the direction that we are getting ready to go. Finally we are told in scripture that Eve ate of the tree, and then gave the fruit to her husband Adam, which shows us that he had to be close by her to receive the fruit and eat it also.

So here would be the last question I have for you on this matter: after Adam saw Eve eat from the forbidden tree, why didn't he correct her and tell her how wrong she was? Instead, he joined Eve in disobeying God. So from the scripture we can see the importance of obeying God when he speaks and tells us to keep – or *shamar* -- our families.

So how does this relate to what we are talking about? Could it be that we have many men and women who are so busy dressing the ministries that God has given unto them that they fail to keep their first ministry, which is to their family? As Adam was going about dressing the garden, working hard to see the garden looking good, he was so busy that he let a serpent spend too much time talking to his wife. Let me stop here and speak to the men of God out there who are so busy dressing their ministries that they don't realize that there is a serpent at their house talking to their wives and children. The enemy is busy telling your wife that she is not loved by you, and that you are in love with another lady called ministry. While the serpent is telling your children to engage in all kinds of ungodly activities, you're so caught up in dressing your lover, the mistress called ministry, that you're losing your family. So I ask you to get home and minister to your family and stop the serpent from talking to your family.

Now on the other hand we have women of God out there preaching at every conference, on every television show they can be on, but then they have natural daughters who need their mom to show them how to be young ladies… but the mother is so busy dressing her garden that she is not paying her daughter any attention. Then you have the husband who is being tempted strongly by the enemy to go outside of his marriage. This is not because he does not love his wife and family, but it is because when it is time for his wife to take time and satisfy his sexual needs, she is too busy dressing her ministry. In the middle of her getting ready to make love to her husband, she gets a call about her website and leaves her husband in the bed unsatisfied. So I say to the women of God, please get home and to care of your daughters, and while you're doing that, please break your husband off a little bit of that Kit-Kat bar so that the serpent that continues to come to the church trying to show him some attention and dressing like you can be put in check.

Please don't do this as a one-time thing, but begin to make this apart of your daily lifestyle. Do not put ministry before your spouse take care of your family needs -- it goes back to what I said earlier: we all need balance. I would like to give some clarity to something I said early about men of God being tempted by the serpent to go outside their marriage. I'm not giving any kind of excuse for men or women to go outside their marriage to be fulfilled in any kind of way, whether it is emotional or sexual. What I'm saying is that you can stop the plan of the enemy by prioritizing your life and making sure that you don't spend so much time dressing your ministry that you can't see the serpent trying to talk to your spouse and to your family. Next I would like to show you the restoration that the last Adam brought to us, because the first Adam failed his assignment.

1 Corinthians 15:45 (King James Version)

[45] And so it is written, The first Adam was made a living soul; the last Adam was a living soul; the last Adam was made a quickening spirit.

This scripture that was written by the Apostle Paul shows us that Adam was called the first Adam and Jesus Christ is the last Adam. With this being said, I would like to bring a little correction to the Body of Christ about Jesus being the second Adam. Nowhere in the scripture do we find that Jesus is called the second Adam: that is something that men have used in their messages, but it is not scriptural. If there was a second Adam, then that means there can be a third, fourth, fifth, and sixth Adam. Jesus was the "last" Adam, which lets us know that there will be no more. With this scripture I would like to begin to bring some revelation concerning the work that Christ accomplished through His death, burial, and resurrection. I have to give you some scriptures here so that you can follow me.

Genesis 2:15 (King James Version)

[15] And the LORD God took the man, and put him into the garden of Eden to dress it and to keep it.

Now you see this scripture again, but now we are going to deal with the part that tells us that God took Adam and put him into the Garden of Eden and gave him a mandate to dress and keep it. We established that Jesus was the last Adam who came to restore back to us what the first Adam lost in the Garden of Eden. We are going to show you a picture of the account in Genesis happening all over again -- this time it is not the first Adam; it is the last Adam.

Matthew 26:36-44 (King James Version)

36 Then cometh Jesus with them unto a placed called Gethsemane, and saith unto the disciples, Sit ye here, while I go and pray yonder.

37 And he took with him Peter and the two sons of Zebedee, and began to be sorrowful and very heavy.

38 Then saith he unto them, My soul is exceeding sorrowful, even unto death: tarry ye here, and watch with me.

39 And he went a little farther, and fell on his face, and prayed, saying, o my father, if it be possible, let this cup pass from me: nevertheless not as I will, but as thou wilt.

40 And he cometh unto the disciples, and findeth them asleep, and saith unto Peter, What, could ye not watch with me one hour?

41 Watch and pray, that ye enter not into temptation: the spirit indeed is willing, but the flesh is weak.

42 He went away again the second time, and prayed, saying O my Father, if this cup may not pass from me, except I

drink it, thy will be done.

[43] And he came and found them asleep again: for their eyes were heavy.

[44] And he left them, and went away again, and prayed the third time, saying the same words.

As we dig into this scripture, we find that Jesus and the disciples are in the garden of Gethsemane, and He tells most of the disciples to sit down while He goes on to pray. We see that Peter and the sons of Zebedee have the chance to walk a little further with Him. The scripture tells us that Jesus begins to be very sorrowful and very heavy. Then Jesus told Peter and the sons of Zebedee to stop at a certain point and to watch with Him. Jesus then falls on His face and begins to seek the face of God about the situation that is soon to occur. The Bible explains to us that Jesus went and prayed three different times to the Father, but in the middle of those different prayer times He started to give His disciples instructions. The point I would like to focus on is the fact that He is in a garden. The reason I would like to focus here is because the first Adam messed up in the garden of Eden, and the last Adam is getting ready to win in the garden of Gethsemane. Jesus was able to keep or *shamar* the garden even though He was experiencing the greatest fight of His life.

Well, what does this have to do with where we are? When you look in Luke 22 you will find that Luke was able to see another side of this story. Luke tells us that Jesus not only prays, but that an angel is sent from heaven to strengthen Him. Luke also shares with us that Jesus was in so much agony that His sweat was like drops of blood. I would like to believe that Jesus at this time had the pressure from the first Adam resting on Him; I believe that Jesus realized that He has to make sure he protected His Bride the church, even in the garden of Gethsemane. Many of you may say that the church was not born yet, but I would like to say that He was carrying His bride inside of Him, like the first Adam was carrying his wife inside of him. We will deal with this a little later to bring a deeper understanding to what I mean by that. This is what I'm saying: I believe that Jesus had to come to a garden to prove to the enemy that even though the first Adam did not fully *shamar* or keep his wife, that He would come back to a garden and make sure that even in the midst of his humanity talking, saying "Father if it be thy will let this cup pass from me, nevertheless not my will but yours be done," Jesus gave every man and woman of God the ability to properly *shamar* their family again. In other words, Jesus did not allow His humanity or the agony He was facing to get Him off track with looking out for His bride who was in Him.

Jesus understood that if He had turned away from the agony, then we the church, or the bride of Christ, would have been messed up. So I say to every man and woman of God that you do not have any excuse to allow ministry to become your mistress. You cannot say that because of what the first Adam did we are doomed, because we are grateful to God the Father for sending the Last Adam who brought restoration back to our families. Let me go back to something I told you earlier in the chapter that we would deal with later, and that is the fact that Jesus was carrying His bride inside of Him, just like Adam carried Eve. To prove this we need more scripture.

Genesis 2:21-22 (King James Version)

[21] And the Lord God caused a deep sleep to fall upon Adam, And he slept: and he took one of his ribs, and closed up the flesh instead thereof

[22] And the rib, which the Lord God had taken from man, made he woman, and brought her onto the man.

This scripture shows us that God caused a deep sleep to fall upon Adam, and after He put Adam to sleep, He took one of his ribs and closed him up so that He could begin to create the woman from the rib that He had taken out of Adam. After God created the woman from Adam's rib, He then presented the woman unto Adam. Now we can understand how Adam had Eve in him all along. I would like to prove to you from the scripture that Jesus had the church in Him, and that is why he did not allow anything to stop Him from being totally obedient to God the Father. Jesus knew that He could not get overly engaged in working miracles and spending time with the disciples that He forgot about His wife that he was carrying, which is the Bride of Christ, the Church. Look at John 19:33-34.

John 19:33-34 (King James Version)

[33] But when they came to Jesus, and saw that he was dead already, they brake not his legs.

[34] But one of the soldiers with a spear pierced his side, and forthwith came there blood and water.

John explains to us what happened at the time that our Lord was being crucified. John is letting us know that when the soldiers came to Jesus and saw he was dead already, that they did not break his legs. But John states that one soldier took a spear and pierced him in his SIDE. What is this all about, I believe, is that just like the first Adam was put into a deep sleep to get Eve out, now Jesus is in a deep sleep so to speak, so that the church could come out. I believe that when the solider pierced Jesus in the side that His wife the church was being now created from out of Him. It was in my view necessary for that to happen as a symbolic act to the first Adam who messed up, and his wife who also messed up. Now through our Lord Jesus Christ, who had His prioritizes together, there was a redeeming to husbands so they can be men of God who keep ministry in the right perspective, and also there was a new wife created called the Bride of Christ, which is you and I who have accepted Jesus as our Lord and Savior. Therefore, like Eve, we are called to be a helpmeet for Jesus in the earth realm, which means we are to co-labour with Him to advance His kingdom in the earth.

I hope by now you can see the revelation that is coming

to you. I know that the garden happened before the crucifixion, which will make it look like what I'm saying is a contradiction, but here is the point: the reason why Christ won in the garden was because He was doing what the first Adam failed at. Jesus protected His wife the church from the personal agony He was facing, and He prayed so that the enemy would have no room to get in and make Him lose sight of protecting, watching over, standing guard over, policing, securing, defending, shielding, sheltering, screening, covering, cloaking, preserving, saving, conserving, supervising, governing, or restraining, His wife, the Bride of Christ, us. So at the end of this chapter I say to you that Christ loved the church so much that He would not allow His work in the ministry stop Him from His true purpose of providing for His Bride.

Here's the answer to our question: is ministry a mistress? No, ministry is not a mistress if put in the proper Godly order. Ministry was given by God for us to enjoy working for Him, and allowing Him to work through us. Ministry becoming a mistress is up to the individual who allows ministry to come before his or her God- ordained responsibilities, which are: God first of course, then your spouse and children. When are you going to stop looking at your marriage just as a marriage, and start to look at it as ministry?

MARRIAGE, YOUR
FIRST MINISTRY

I hope and pray that you are receiving some strength through what you are reading that will help you become balanced and become a better husband to your wife, or a better wife to your husband. Let's look at how marriage becomes your first ministry and the mistress has no room, when we have this understanding that marriage is also ministry.

We are all familiar with the idea that we are Christ's body on earth—His hands, His feet. It is through us that He reaches out to the world. But it's easy to forget that we are Christ's hands and feet to our spouse. That's why seeing your marriage as ministry may require an intentional shift of perspective.

Your marriage is not something that you can compartmentalize as having less priority in giving your attention to it, in light of your ministry to your church family.

It is clear in Scripture that the Holy Spirit specifically appoints certain men and women as leaders by gifting them and putting it in their hearts to serve joyfully in the context of a local church (Acts 20:28; cf. 1 Timothy 3:1). It's a noble desire. It can be an all-consuming desire. But, with this desire comes the responsibility to humbly prioritize one's life in such a way that prevents a subtle disregard for God's written word. God has not commanded husbands to love ministry more than their wives. He has commanded that we love our wives and strive to protect our marriages, even from something as noble as our ministry call.

In this context, your marriage is more important to tend to and keep healthy than even your apostolic or pastoral ministry outside of your home, because you are representing Christ to your bride (just as Christ is the bridegroom to the church, His bride).

As we looked at earlier, every Christian marriage holds that "great mystery" (see: Ephesians 5:21-33). When you are married, you became covenant partners with your spouse and with God to help address each other's aloneness. Your spouse, above other human beings, is to be your ministry focus because of the vows you made when you married. God Himself acknowledged from the beginning that "it is not good for man to be alone." He said this even though He was walking and fellowshipping with man.

God knew that there are certain emotional and temporal needs that a human being —a marriage partner -- is created to meet. And there are certain emotional and temporal needs that you are created to meet for your marriage partner. "And the two shall be one."

That is part of your role in the covenant of marriage. It is a cord of three strands, with God being involved right from the start.

Problems can arise, however, when men and women forget or overlook the importance of the partnership of marriage, which he or she entered into with his/her spouse.

I'm not implying that you are together only to meet emotional and temporal needs, but I'm saying that is a part of the bigger plan to please your spouse: emotionally, temporally, and of course spiritually.

Marriage and Ordination

The rite of ordination does not override the rite of marriage. Both are noble callings, and one is not the "higher calling." Both were instituted by God for the sanctification of His people.

You made the choice to go into the ministry. And with that choice came certain "duties and obligations." You also made the choice to marry. And with that choice, certain "duties and obligations" came with it as well. Your options changed as far as how much time you can devote to the ministry apart from your spouse and keep your relationship healthy and strong —one that strongly reflects the love relationship between the Bridegroom (Christ) and His Bride —which is what every Christian marriage is supposed to represent.

When you were unmarried, you had the freedom to be "undivided" in the attention you could dedicate to the Lord's work. But in <u>1 Corinthians 7</u>, the Apostle Paul warns you are to realize that things change once you marry. And as he said,

1 Corinthians 7:32-34 (King James Version)

[32]But I would have you without carefulness. He that is unmarried careth for the things that belong to the Lord, how he may please the Lord:

[33]But he that is married careth for the things that are of the world, how he may please his wife.

[34]There is difference also between a wife and a virgin. The unmarried woman careth for the things of the Lord, that she may be holy both in body and in spirit: but she that is married careth for the things of the world, how she may please her husband.

When you marry, your ministry becomes divided between ministering within the home and outside of the home. *BOTH* become your concern and your focus at this point.

But keep in mind that this doesn't mean that your ministry is lessened; it just means that it is redirected so that not only do you minister outside of your home, but also within it as well. You represent Christ to your bride, so don't forget the calling of your ministry with your wife and family.

Please read

Ephesians 5:24-33 (King James Version)

Verse 31- For this reason shall a man leave his father and mother, and be joined unto his wife, and the two shall become one flesh. Verse 32 -This is a great mystery: but I speak concerning Christ and the church. Verse 33- nevertheless let every one of you in particular so love his wife even as himself; and the wife see that she reverence her husband. *(Ephesians 5:24-33)*.

I say to you again, men of God, not only is it important to love your wife "as Christ loves the church and gave himself up for her," because you have entered into covenant with her and with God, but also so that you don't bruise her emotionally. Your spouse should not be any less important than others that you minister to outside of the home. When you hurt her, or neglect her, how will you be able to "present her" to God "as a radiant church, without spot or wrinkle or any other blemish"?

Keep in mind that your marriage is a living example of Christ's love for the church, both within your home and outside of it. As others observe how you treat your wife or husband, the love of the Lord should be evident. It gives the Lord the opportunity to draw others to Himself as they observe your behavior. It's another evangelistic vehicle that the Lord can use as you avail yourself.

Something that Ravi Zacharias said, in his book, *I, Isaac, Take Thee, Rebekah: Moving from Romance to Lasting Love* is relevant to your calling in considering your marriage as a ministry and as an evangelistic "tool." He wrote:

"Some time ago, I was lecturing at a major university and by the tremendous response both in the numbers of students attending the sessions and in their questions, it was evident to all that God was at work.

"As the man who had organized the event drove me to the airport, he said something that was quite jolting to me. He said, 'My wife brought our neighbor last night. She is a medical doctor and had not been to anything like this before. On their way home, my wife asked her what she thought of it all.' He stopped and there was silence in the van for a moment. He continued, 'She said, "That was a very powerful evening. The arguments were very persuasive. I wonder what he is like in his private life."'

"I have to admit it was one of the most sobering things I had ever heard. She was right. Did these lofty truths apply in private as well as in public discourse?

"The truth is that God calls us to first practice truth in private so that its public expression is merely an outgrowth of what has already taken place in the heart and not a decoration over a hollow life. Developing that strength of character in private is foundational."

That is a very powerful article. From it, we can glean that

this is why you need to understand that your marriage is another vehicle that God wants to use to draw others to Himself. Marriage is the foundation of family life, and marriage is one of God's greatest tools for ministry. Let me say that again: marriage is one of God's greatest tools for ministry. My goal isn't to build stronger marriages. It's to build stronger marriages for a purpose — ministry.

The purpose is so that when others see how we interact with each other in ways that display the love of God, it could very well attract them to our lives, our homes, and ultimately to want to know our God better. And isn't that the point of the ministry that God has called you to, as a leader?

Men of God act out the Gospel as they sacrificially love their wives even as Christ loved the church and gave Himself up for her. Likewise, women of God too act out that Gospel as they, in Christian love and devotion, submit to their husbands even as the church submits to her Lord.

The important practical application of all this is that each of us needs to make it a high priority to love and cherish our spouses. The best way to defend our church body from error is to proclaim the Scriptures boldly and to love our spouses nobly. By strengthening our own marriages, we set an example for the entire church and make it that much harder for the devil to break through our ranks.

Make sure you strengthen your marriage behind closed

doors and in front of open ones as well. How much of a "ministry" do you really have going on, when you aren't ministering to the needs of your spouse?

Always remember that God doesn't desire your ministry to become a mistress. So do yourself a favor and cultivate your marriage behind closed doors because "your Father who sees in secret will reward you." (Matthew 6:4)

I pray you will prayerfully consider these points, examine your marriage, and ask the Lord to show you anything that you may or may not be doing that needs to be corrected in the present and future. You may want to pray what the psalmist prayed in Psalm 139:23-24

[23] Search me O God and know my heart, try me and know my thoughts.

[24] See if there be any wicked way in me, and lead me in the way everlasting

Ministry Shall Not Destroy Your Marriage

In this chapter I would like to share how my heart was heavy several years ago, before I even got married. You will find out that even though I went into my marriage with a mindset not to allow what I have seen to become the state of my marriage. I found out quickly that I begin to have some of the same traits that I believe destroy a lot of kingdom marriages. Well, how did this happen? I allowed myself to be seduced by the mistress called ministry. It was not ministry in and of itself, but I became so focused on building ministry that I was neglecting my first ministry to my very own wife. But thank God for His grace and for His convictions. I'm also grateful that I had a heart to receive the correction of the Holy Spirit. One of the things that really began to bother me as I was on this journey was the fact that I heard many men and women of God saying how they travel so much because both of them were in the ministry. The problem I had with this was that they would get on television and say because of their great traveling schedules, they would see each other only once or twice a week. Now to me this is not balance -- this is the way that you give the enemy room to get into your marriage, because you're consumed with ministry. Let me inject here that ministry shall not destroy your marriage. So as you read this portion of the book, it may seem I going backwards in the story, but that is not what I'm doing. My purpose in sharing some of the thoughts my wife and I now had is to show you how you can have great intentions and great hopes to not allow ministry to be a mistress, but then you realize it is not about talking it out, it's about walking it out. Let look at some scripture to see what God feels about us letting things separate our marriages.

Mark 10:9 (King James Version)

⁹What therefore God hath joined together, let not man put asunder.

Understanding this scripture it lets us know that whatever God puts together, let no man put asunder. So we need to understand that we can't let the people we serve in the work of ministry pull our marriages apart because of the demands that they may put on you. Those of you whom God has joined together by His Spirit cannot afford to let the pressures and the responsibilities of ministry draw your attention away from your spouse.

The stress couples face in ministry tears some marriages apart. But there are things you can do to make

both your marriage and ministry successful. I declare that ministry shall not destroy your marriage.

As news of the third breakup of a marriage and ministry within a year's time came to my attention, I suddenly felt vulnerable. Even though I was not directly related to any of these newly broken marriages, I somehow felt emotionally betrayed by their delinquency in their marriage vows.

I had not been married yet; I was soon to be married and had been the apostle of All Nations Evangelistic Church for two years. I emotionally identified with them -- not in marriage, but in the challenge that I felt that can come to marriages that are in the ministry. Even though I refused to set myself up as a judge, I was still hurt by the impact of the loss of these marriages and their ministries to the Christian community.

These leaders were of significant prominence in our nation within the ranks of Christianity. Each of these marriages had lasted twenty years or more. As a young man of God I felt stunned, yet I determined that such an outcome would not be the case with my marriage.

But what were my future wife and I to do? We certainly didn't perceive ourselves as being any more spiritual or gifted than these fallen leaders. If they could not succeed, what should we glean from these situations?

As we pondered these questions and more, my fiancée and I began to ask ourselves: (1) how do the mighty fall? And (2) how can we not only survive but also enjoy the journey? Following are some of the answers we discovered:

Ministry places marriages under stress. It is important to understand the nature of ministry itself. People in ministry tend to be consumed with vision. In Psalm 69:9 David proclaims, "For the zeal of thine hath eaten me up." (KJV) Close behind this is busy-ness. Ministers of the gospel are easily consumed with activity and good deeds.

If this is not balanced with some times of relaxation, tiredness and discouragement can settle into the soul, causing a loss of perspective. This is followed by a loss of purpose, which then births spiritual weariness. If the spiritually weary minister does not receive refreshing, then not only is the "whole man" affected, but also the ministry and the marriage.

Although there is nothing wrong with working until you get tired, constant tiredness easily turns into discouragement and weariness, and that is not the will of God.

How do the mighty fall? The following is an all-too-typical pattern:

The husband desires respect and intimacy, and the wife desires provision and cherishing.

Expectations are disappointed.

Loss of respect for one another occurs.

Lack of gratefulness sets in.

Resistance to sexual intimacy follows.

Estimation of personal worth comes into question.

There are surface attempts to improve matters, but transparency remains awkward and difficult.

Disappointment and resentment build.

The wife tires of his vision or lack of it and becomes lackadaisical or ambivalent. The husband buries himself in the work of his ministry or wearily gives up altogether.

Loss of hope for the marriage and/or ministry occurs.

When brokenness occurs in a marriage, pain and loss always follow. A marriage is never an island unto itself. There are always family members and friends who are affected by the success or failure of every marriage. A ministry marriage has an even greater ripple effect on the lives of people, not only because of its position, but also because of its message.

Marriage is a covenant. Not only is a ministry marriage under view of the public eye, the message of covenant commitment that it proclaims is as well. Whether the United States is still a nation that fulfills the "in God we trust" message of its currency or not, it is still a nation that puts unspoken demands on its ministers. It is a nation that expects its ministers to either demonstrate the power of covenant commitment in their marriages, or quit talking about it.

Covenant in the Scripture is very significant. When God made a covenant with Abraham in Genesis 15, He had Abraham sacrifice animals by cutting them into two pieces and then had a smoking firepot with a blazing torch appear and pass between the two pieces. Covenant-making was so important to God that He demonstrated its importance with the price of shed blood.

In Jeremiah 34, after King Zedekiah had made a covenant with the people of Jerusalem to set his Jewish slaves free and then broke that covenant, God brought judgment to him. In verse 18 God said through Jeremiah: "The men who have violated my covenant and have not fulfilled the terms of the covenant they made before me, I will treat like the calf they cut in two and then walked between its pieces." In other words, because they broke their covenant promises, they were going to die.

When a man and a woman come together in marriage, the vows they make to one another are of great significance. They are covenant vows of promise. In essence, as they come to the altar and present their vows to one another, they are saying, "May I be as a dead animal if I do not keep my promises to you."

Just as Christ shed His blood for the sake of the new covenant, we make the marriage vow "until death parts us." Even though some do not understand God's Word on the issue of covenant, they do look for the fruit of it from ministers.

The pressure of public scrutiny -- the realization of a

watchful eye -- can put pressure on any marriage, but the awareness of an ever-watchful eye by family members and society at large can most certainly put a burden on a ministry marriage.

So in the midst of it all, how can we as ministers of the gospel guard our marriages without bending to performance pressure? How can we bear up under the pressure of living in a glass house and not lose sight of the joy in marriage as God intended?

The answer is simple: We are to walk out the plan and destiny God has for every marriage, and nothing more. In other words, we are to "practice what we preach." As you well know, this is much easier to preach, counsel, and write about than it is to live.

Integrate, don't isolate. This is one of the primary keys to guarding your marriage. You must integrate your attitudes, schedules, and activities. If you don't, the church can emotionally become like "the other woman" in the life of your marriage. I have rarely met a spouse who wants to fight "with God" over time demands.

Usually when one partner is overly involved in church business that is disconnected from their spouse on a consistent basis, that spouse feels taken advantage of, becomes resentful toward the church, and simply withdraws. They feel guilty for their resentment because it seems as though they are in competition with God for their spouse's attention.

They often struggle with their emotions and have difficulty separating God from the church and their partner's overindulgence in activity. So they begin to emotionally withdraw. When this happens, the lure of another person slipping in and meeting their relational desires becomes easier to succumb to than they ever imagined it would.

Separating emotionally from marriage and ministry is dangerous, and sadly often leads to a spiritual separation. The partner who is emotionally less involved may begin to question their personal spirituality and withdraw into a survival mode. After all, who wants to "compete with God?" This imagined competition occurs usually because of a misperception of the value of the gifts that God has given to each individual, and how those gifts are being used.

I strongly believe, however, that God calls each of us individually to do a work for Him according to the unique gifts He has given us.

Every minister's wife or husband should attend church because he or she wants to gather with other believers and give worship to God, not because his or her spouse is the minister. They should reach out with their unique gifts and talents and serve God's people because we're all called to be servants, not because they are trying to live up to some preconceived notion of what a minister's wife or husband should be. Always remember that God wants you to work together in your marriage, and then in the work of the ministry. So again I say that ministry shall not destroy your marriage.

MARRIED AND
IN THE MINISTRY

In this chapter I would like to take the time to deal with the other side of being married and in the ministry. I understand that by now many of you are getting the point of what is being said. There are some great benefits to being married to someone who understands ministry, because they also have a strong mandate upon their life as well. I have come to realize the great strength that my wife carries out in the ministry. I have come to understand the strength it takes from a spouse to be able to hold up under such a mandate from God. I'm sure my wife will say the same; being married to someone that is also called to ministry is a joyous thing. I can truly say that there is nothing like having a woman of God beside me in the work of ministry, who keeps me balanced. In times of great warfare there is nothing like having a partner who can flow prophetically and speak the word of the Lord. There have been many days when my wife has been an encouraging force in the midst of trials that all leaders face. The flip side to everything is that I enjoy being a husband who can release apostolic impartation into my wife, it feels great to sit in service and watch how God uses my wife, without any jealousy, because she is a reflection of who I am. So I would like to take just a little time in this chapter to show you what happens when you have a good marriage and the things you can expect from God.

If you sell your family cheaply, people will buy you without payment – African Proverb.

Ecclesiastes 4:8-12 (King James Version)

[8]There is one alone, and there is not a second; yea, he hath neither child nor brother: yet is there no end of all his labor; neither is his eye satisfied with riches; neither saith he, For whom do I labour, and bereave my soul of good? This is also vanity, yea, it is a sore travail.

[9]Two are better than one; because they have a good reward for their labour.

[10]For if they fall, the one will lift up his fellow: but woe to him that is alone when he falleth; for he hath not another to help him up.

[11]Again, if two lie together, then they have heat: but how can one be warm alone?

[12]And if one prevail against him, two shall withstand him; and a threefold cord is not quickly broken.

The impact of a good marriage on ministerial success cannot be overemphasized. When a minister's marriage is bad, it limits his effectiveness and efficiency, stops his upward movement, destroys his inner strength, and creates room for the enemies to attack his anointing. If a wall is not cracked, penetration will be impossible for reptiles. A cracked wall is a room for all manner of spirits.

According to this scripture, we see that Solomon believed that two are better than one, because together they have a good reward for their labour. In other words, something great comes out of married couples in the ministry when they are working together -- you need to understand that it is a blessing to have a spouse that can work with you in the things of the Lord. There is such a reward that will bless cities, regions, and nations of the world because of your labor of love. Also, he lets us know that is it good to have a partner, because if one faints the other can pick him up. How many of you that are married out there can thank God for that? It will be many days that the Lord will use your spouse to speak over you so that you can move on in the things of the Lord.

1 Peter 3:7 (King James Version)

[7]Likewise, ye husbands, dwell with them according to knowledge, giving honour unto the wife, as unto the weaker vessel, and as being heirs together of the grace of life; that your prayers be not hindered.

Answered Prayers

The Apostle Peter tells us to honor our wives, because we are heirs together of the grace of life. Because when we respect our wives, our prayers will not be hindered. Here is one of the benefits to having a great marriage: with a great marriage you have the ability to get prayers answered quickly and more successfully. I have found out that many people who are in the ministry think they can bypass their spouse and go to God in prayer. But we understand that the Bible tells us to be angry but sin not. So it is ok to have disagreements, but don't allow them to become prolonged by anger. The Bible also says that anger rests in the bosom of a fool. So be sure to communicate with your spouse and get things right before you try to jump in God's face with unresolved problems. All I'm saying to you is that if you desire quick answers to your prayers in ministry, then you must stay in unity with your spouse and work on your marriage.

Ecclesiastes 4:12 (King James Version)

¹²And if one prevail against him, two shall withstand him; and a threefold cord is not quickly broken.

Next we see that a threefold cord is not easily broken. This is great to know -- that you your spouse and God are a threefold cord that cannot easily be broken. This means that with your spouse and God, anything is possible. So I would like to say to you that if God puts a dream in your heart to transform nations and you don't have anyone but your spouse, it can and will be done. We need to understand that wherever the presence of God is, there is liberty. So it is such a push for a marriage to understand that if God be for them, He is more than the world against them. Don't go without the presence of God in your marriage. The greatest need of every minister is the presence of God. A bad marriage repels God's presence, while a good marriage encourages it. God will never dwell in confusion. You will always find Him in a place of order. Orderliness is the order of the day in His kingdom. Any minister that desires His presence should work on his/her marriage.

As you create an environment of peace in your marriage, it will help you in the ministry. Some may say, "How will creating peace in my marriage help me in the ministry?" It will help you to remove loneliness; apostolic and prophetic work can be lonely at times. There are many times when you are pioneering present truth into a region where you might be misunderstood, misquoted, and mistreated, but when you have a spouse, who has clarity of the call and supports you and ministers to you, and you also minister to them in times of attack, it will remove loneliness. Sometimes, church members may not understand how you feel, and may not be there for you. In fact, if they can't take the heat they may jump out the pot. The danger in this case is to have a bad marriage because that is going to be an extra pressure for you. I don't know of any leader who wants to war with the enemy in the city, region, nations and in the lives of believers they oversee, and then get home and have to put another war suit on because they are warring with their spouse.

I would like to speak for a moment to every cutting-edge leader who is not willing to settle for the mundane, but who desires the miraculous. Please begin now gathering the intercessors to pray for your marriage every day. Why? Because the enemy does not like the fact that you are helping people's lives; therefore he would like to send demonic attacks against your marriage. I feel like making a apostolic decree right here: I decree and declare that your marriage shall be strong in the Lord in the power of His might. I decree that your marriage will make it through every test sent against it. I decree that your marriage will be used to bring transformation, reformations, revival, renewal, and restoration to the nations of the world in JESUS' NAME. Receive that right now while you're reading this book. I would like you right now to take a moment and begin to praise God for your marriage. If you are not married, I want you to praise God for the mighty man or woman of God that is coming your way -- do it right now and then pick the book back up.

The next thing is progress: when there is good marriage, a ministry can progress. When there is open conflict in the life of leaders, that can become a hindrance to their ministry. So it is safe to say that good marriage leads to good ministries. If you would ask any man or woman of God who is having great breakthrough in ministry, what is their secret to success, what would they say? We already know a Godly lifestyle, purity, honesty, and holiness, are the way leaders should live, so we are not going to focus on this part. I believe they would say good marriage is a key to what they are able to do in the kingdom. As I'm writing this book, there are so many great things that God is doing for our ministry. But I would have to say that it is so easy to flow in what God is doing because I have a wife who has a heart to see God's kingdom advance more and more. I can honestly say that my wife has always been a great support to the work of the Lord. As I see God raising my wife to be and Apostolic Prophet to the nations, I can easily say that she will be able to progress in the call of God. I take the responsibility as her husband first to pray for her and to make sure that I speak into her life every chance I get. So the benefit of having a good marriage is that you can watch each other grow in the things of God together, and you can see the different dimensions that the Holy Spirit will take you both as one, when there is unity in the marriage.

When there is a good marriage you can find strength. Let's look at Ecclesiastes again: And if one prevail against him, two shall withstand him; and a threefold cord is not quickly broken. Ecclesiastes 4:12 (King James Version) spiritually, emotionally, physically, and financially, good marriage leads to strength and formidability. It helps during spiritual warfare, financial needs, sickness, challenges, church crisis, etc. You find that in warfare you and your spouse become an army. What one of you could not take down, when both of you come together in agreement, something happens in the realm of the Spirit. Look at what the gospel of Matthew says concerning this:

Matthew 18:18-20 (King James Version)

[18]Verily I say unto you, Whatsoever ye shall bind on earth shall be bound in heaven: and whatsoever ye shall loose on earth shall be loosed in heaven.

[19]Again I say unto you, That if two of you shall agree on earth as touching any thing that they shall ask, it shall be done for them of my Father which is in heaven.

[20]For where two or three are gathered together in my name, there am I in the midst of them.

I will say the next benefit you receive from a good marriage is support. Again, if two lie together, then they have heat: but how can one be warm alone? (Eccl. 4:11) Good marriage is a source of support for ministers. It makes you warm in time of cold conditions. There is no war greater than "inner war." No support is better than that which comes from your spouse. There is so much support that comes to a leader when they can go home and express the battle they have been facing all day, and have a spouse there who supports them by uplifting them, reaffirming to them that God is going to do what He promised.

Numbers 23:19 (King James Version)

[19]God is not a man, that he should lie; neither the son of man, that he should repent: hath he said, and shall he not do it? or hath he spoken, and shall he not make it good?

When you have a great spouse who is also in the ministry, you can focus. Good marriage allows you to focus on ministry without any distractions from your spouse because your marriage is built in such a strong way. Good marriage is good ministry; when you have a bad marriage, then it begins to hurt your ministry. People don't understand that preachers go through things just like everyone else, so therefore there is always a higher expectation from saints and from sinners for preachers' marriages. Great marriage allows you to focus together on the assignment of God; it also gives you the ability to be free from the burden of a bad marriage. We must understand that a bad marriage is the greatest source of distraction for any minister.

1 Timothy 3

[1]This is a true saying, if a man desire the office of a bishop, he desireth a good work.

[2]A bishop then must be blameless, the husband of one wife, vigilant, sober, of good behaviour, given to hospitality, apt to teach;

[3]Not given to wine, no striker, not greedy of filthy lucre;

but patient, not a brawler, not covetous;

4One that ruleth well his own house, having his children in subjection with all gravity;

5(For if a man know not how to rule his own house, how shall he take care of the church of God?)

6Not a novice, lest being lifted up with pride he fall into the condemnation of the devil.

7Moreover he must have a good report of them which are without; lest he fall into reproach and the snare of the devil.

As we look at 1Timothy 3:1-7 we understand that credibility is part of a good marriage. This scripture speaks to men and women who would like to be leaders in God's church. Usually people read this scripture from a traditional view; they always see "a bishop" from the traditional view instead of a true Biblical view. When a leader has good family credibility and they are in great standing with their spouse and children that will enhance a ministry. Good marriage is the first qualification for any leadership office. Bad marriage, bad ministry; good marriage, good ministry. If you want to be a credible minister, it starts from your marriage. The home front is the real front of your ministry. It is not a collar that brings credibility, but a good companion. You can NEVER rise beyond the level of your marriage. When you have your home in order, you can expect the blessings of the Lord to come upon your house and the ministry that He has called you to.

If you build a strong marriage, then in return you will have a blessed family. If you want good children, build a good marriage. Good marriage helps in the raising of children. Statistics show that most prostitutes, area boys, cultists, armed robbers, drug addicts and other nonentities are from very bad homes. Victor Hugo says, "He who opens a school closes a prison." I have found that many preachers' kids are caught up in a lot of ungodly lifestyles because they have seen their parents preach one thing from behind the pulpit at church and live another thing at home. So if you build a strong marriage, then your children will see what a marriage that is in ministry is supposed to look like. I don't want to get caught here, but there are many wounded preachers' children who desire healing but they don't know who to talk to. I will deal with this in another book that the Holy Spirit has laid on my heart to write.

One of the great benefits from a good marriage is church growth: when people see that it is possible for God to use couples, they are encouraged to seek God to also bless their marriage. I have found out that many people will not come to your church if they know you have a bad home. Therefore, good marriage is another good way to grow your church. The reason why people are looking for strong marriages is because they are battling to maintain theirs, and they would like someone who can minister to them. I prophetically declare that this is the time that God is raising kingdom couples to go forth in the ministry together like never before. We will begin to see strong Aquila and Priscilla-like marriages who will travel the world upgrading people apostolically like this couple did in the Book of Acts.

Last but not least, I believe that good marriage guards against immorality. Good marriage helps to avoid sexual sins. When a man is satisfied with fried rice, he is not likely to steal someone else's popcorn. When a man or woman is fulfilled at home, it becomes harder for the enemy to get in and cause an affair. Work on your marriage. NO MATRIMONY, NO MINISTRY. Give God a room in your ministry by creating a home for Him in your Marriage. Remember – The home front is the real front of your ministry.

In the next few pages I would like to give some motivating keys to couples in the ministry. I believe these keys will be beneficial to you in having a great marriage in the ministry. It will also give you the courage to thank God for the difference that He has placed in your spouse's life. God has put you together for His plans -- don't let any man put you asunder. If you take these keys and apply them to your marriage, you will function in marriage and ministry fulfilled all the days of your life.

MOTIVATING KEYS FOR MINISTRY COUPLES

Staying in covenant with one another requires that a ministry couple remain connected. Following are eight motivating keys to building strong relationships in ministry:

1. **Appreciate the differences**. The differences between the two of you may be in personality type, gifts, talents, or seasons of life. But learn to appreciate and enjoy the way God made your partner. Benefit from the differences. Even though you may have different gifts and functions within the church, your hearts should remain intertwined.

One of you may have a more public ministry, while the other may minister more effectively to individuals in private conversation. The point is not in the how, but in your hearts staying intertwined and ministering together. One may be responsible for decisions on huge money matters and building projects, while the other is focused on children's soccer schedules and music lessons; but the desire and the effort to stay connected is essential. Sometimes these differences are seasonal, as with the raising of children, but they need to be appreciated and respected.

2. **Don't compare**. Don't compare your spouse's gifts with someone else's in a similar capacity. We preach to the church not to compare themselves with each other, but sometimes we secretly long for our spouse to function like another person we admire in a similar ministry. This is easily discerned and will cause deep wounds in our relationship. Those wounds tear the shield-guard from the marriage.

3. **Honor one another**. Ephesians 5:21 encourages believers to "submit to one another out of reverence for Christ." Paul then proceeds to tell wives to respect and submit to

THE MISTRESS CALLED MINISTRY

their husbands, and husbands to love their wives. As the leaders in the church, if we do not walk in humility and honor one another, what kind of message does that send to those watching?

The story is told of Queen Victoria and Prince Albert long ago. They had a quarrel one day, and Albert stormed off to his bedroom. The Queen followed in quick pursuit, knocked on the door and demanded, "Albert, it's the Queen of England, I demand that you let me in!" There was no response.

Once again, she banged on the door proclaiming, "Albert, this is the Queen, let me in at once!" There was no response from behind the closed door.

With a third approach, she softly knocked on the door with a beseeching request, "Albert, this is Victoria; I'd really like to speak with you. May I come in?" At once, the closed door was opened.

Whether you're a senior pastor or a prince, every man appreciates the respect of the recognition of his God-ordained headship role, and every woman appreciates the love and honor that is due her according to the Word of God. Each partner responds to humility and an honoring approach. We must not forget who we are and who we are not. Just as the Scripture requires of elders not to be harsh in their ruling manner (see 1 Tim. 3), so husbands and wives -- especially those in leadership roles -- should treat one another with honor and humility.

4. **Be loyal**. The Old English definition of "friend" is "a second in a duel." A "second" was a person who would stand alongside of you if you were in a fight to the death. In fact, if you did not show up, the second would fight the duel for you, risking his life on your behalf.

One of the ways that ministry marriage partners can be loyal to each other is to be loyal in word, action, and heart. Neither spouse should complain about the other to other people, nor should they ever belittle them in front of others. Doing this undermines their authority and respect in the congregation.

Not only is remaining faithful to your covenant important, but appearing to remain faithful to it is important as well. In other words, you should be careful about your personal involvement with others, and never behave in such a way as would cause an onlooker to wonder about your faithfulness to your spouse. You should also constantly be thoughtful of your spouse's schedule and be willing to adapt and adjust, blend and integrate.

Perhaps the most important aspect of loyalty is that of the heart. Proverbs 4:23 says, "Above all else, guard your heart, for it is the wellspring of life."

Ministers are not exempt from the attacks of the enemy, nor are they exempt from carnal lusts of the mind. If you find yourself struggling to remain loyal in your heart to your spouse, a time of spiritual fasting before the Lord may be in order. Biblical fasting brings the soul under submission to the spirit and requires it to line up with the Word of God. Other personal disciplines should be considered in this case as well, such as focusing on your spouse's good attributes, not allowing yourself distractions of the fleshly nature, and focusing your mind on the Word of God in prayer.

5. **Cherish the intimacy in your marriage**. Love is not just spoken; it is communicated and demonstrated. Titus 2:4 says that wives should love their husbands; this means that a wife should be an active "husband lover."

Ephesians 5:25 tells husbands to love their wives, meaning that he also should be an active "wife lover." In the midst of all the busy-ness of ministry involvement, we should be very careful to connect throughout the day and speak in terms of endearment to one another.

We should also reserve enough energy for one another to have meaningful intimacy. A meaningful, cherishing sexual relationship nurtures the marriage and the ministry, and it helps to release each partner to minister to others in confidence of their spouse's undivided love and desire to be intimate in spirit, soul, and body.

6. **Be spiritually attentive to one another**. Learn how to draw out one another's spiritual potential -- but remember that pressure can stifle personal sharing in this area.

Don't expect your spouse to pray with you the way that another minister says it works in his or her marriage. Let your spouse be who they are, and don't force a predefined role on them. You have accepted them in other areas of their personality, so you should also accept them in the areas of personal and privately shared devotions.

7. **Make happy memories**. One of the keys to longevity in marriage and ministry is to make happy memories together. These should be memories that range from intimate moments that no one but you and your spouse will ever know about, to those memories you can "shout from the rooftops" to be a blessing and example to others.

8. **Remember romance**. Cultivating a deeply romantic marriage and ministry partnership with your spouse may be one of the most challenging things you'll ever do, but it will also be one of the most rewarding. Be a serious-minded co-partner when things in life are serious, and laugh and have fun when they are not. Stir your love toward one another and the Lord in some unique way each day.

By taking these important steps, you will not only guard your marriage, but also you will balance your marriage and ministry. Cherish every moment, and build for the future.

REMEMBER YOUR MARRIAGE HAS BEEN MADE IN HEAVEN

Marriage Confessions

My marriage is blessed. My spouse and I are led by the Spirit of God. When we pray together in unity, our prayers are powerful and we get results. We make every effort to establish peace and harmony in our home. Together we walk in agreement and are an unstoppable force.

If we get angry, we are quick to forgive so that we do not have strife in our relationship. We are not self-seeking, rude, proud, boastful, or jealous. Instead, we are loving, kind, patient, and we put each other's needs before our own. We trust each other and protect the sanctity of our marriage. God joined us together as one, and we will not be separated.

Confession References: Deuteronomy 28:1-14, Romans 8:14, Matthew 18:19, I Peter 3:7, Mark 11:25, Romans 13:13, I Corinthians 13:4-8, Matthew 19:6

Your marriage has the potential to bless both you and your spouse in significant ways. So don't settle for less than the best in your marriage. Go after the best God has for you and your spouse by praying big prayers for your marriage.

Here's how:

Be specific. Rather than praying general, vague prayers such as "Lord, please bless our marriage," present specific requests to God. The more you focus your prayers, the more direct responses you'll receive.

Be bold. <u>Jesus</u> emphasized the importance of approaching God with confidence, asking boldly for what you'd like. Don't be timid when you pray for your marriage. Remember that God wants to give you good gifts that are in line with His will. Don't just pray to get by; pray to thrive in your marriage. Go ahead and ask God to do whatever you'd like Him to do in your marriage.

Love Jesus first. Make your relationship with Jesus your top priority -- over your marriage – and encourage your spouse to do the same. If you both make Jesus your first love, His love will fill your marriage and empower you to love each other more. Be sure to look to God for your security and self-esteem – not your spouse. Don't expect your spouse to do what only God can do. Pray for both you and your spouse to have the wisdom and strength to rely on God every day, rather than putting unnecessary pressure on each other.

Pray for emotional intimacy. Ask God to make your marriage a safe relationship and help you and your spouse cultivate openness, honesty, and trust. Confess your sins and talk to God about your deepest fears and longings. Pray for God to heal the emotional wounds that may have damaged your ability to be authentic. Ask God to help you and your spouse enjoy meaningful and intimate conversations.

Pray for spiritual intimacy. Pray that both you and your spouse will constantly seek God's presence and power in your marriage. Ask God to unify you with Him and each other. Pray for protection from distractions that could interfere with you and your spouse seeking God with your whole hearts. Encourage each other to pursue God first before all else. Make a regular practice of praying together, incorporating prayer into your marriage frequently.

Submit to one another out of reverence for Jesus. Ask God to humble you and help you yield to your spouse as a way of honoring Him. Pray for the discernment to know when to defer to your spouse in the decisions that affect both of your lives. Ask God for enough <u>faith</u> to let God deal with the implications of your spouse's decisions – including the bad ones. Ask God to help you find ways to serve your spouse. Pray for the ability to respect your spouse. Ask God to give your spouse appropriate and healthy desires, and to give you a willing spirit so you can yield joyfully. Pray for the Holy Spirit to fill both of you anew on a daily basis.

Pray for your husband. Pray that your husband will: love the Bible and read it regularly, hate sin, love to pray, welcome Christian community in his life and be accountable to at least one Christian man, love to worship, understand the significance of fighting for his family spiritually, be a mighty man of God. Ask God to fill your husband with the Holy Spirit each day and make him a great leader in your marriage.

Pray for your wife. Ask for the grace to treat your wife as well as Jesus treats you. Pray for the humility you need to be a gentle leader in your marriage. Pray for peace in your home, and maturity for you and your wife as you deal with your disagreements. Ask God to strengthen your wife's faith; help her love to pray, worship, and read the Bible, convict her of sin and make her quick to repent, and help her follow where He is leading you both in your marriage. Pray for the ability to see your wife as God sees her and appreciate the gift she is to you.

Pray for your unbelieving spouse. If your spouse is not yet a Christian, ask God to show your spouse his or her need for Jesus. Pray for God to deliver your spouse from evil that deceives him or her, and help your spouse to discover the truth of the Gospel, which will set him or her free. Pray that the way you live out your faith will be a good example to your spouse that will help him or her draw closer to Jesus. Ask God to give your spouse an unmistakable encounter with the Holy Spirit. Pray for Christian friends for your spouse who can influence them in positive ways. Never stop praying for your spouse's salvation as long as he or she is alive!

Pray for protection. Ask God to protect your marriage

from evil influences and temptations that can pull you and your spouse away from Him and each other. Pray for the discernment you need to deal wisely with challenging situations. Find Bible verses that describe the kind of home you want to have, and pray them regularly. Pray against temptations like pornography that can destroy your marriage. Ask God to help you and your spouse manage your time well so you can protect your time together. Pray for you and your spouse to be able to forgive each other quickly when you do make mistakes, so no bitterness will develop between you.

Pray for your marriage's mission. Ask God for the ability to see beyond just the two of you to the greater world and how your marriage can be a blessing in it. Ask God to use your marriage to touch other people's lives in positive ways, contributing to God's kingdom on earth. Pray for a vision of how God wants to use you and your spouse to serve others. Ask God to show you a group of people, a part of the world, or an area of life that you and your spouse are both passionate about and could impact together. Then ask God to lead you to a ministry opportunity in that area. Commit your marriage fully to God and ask Him to constantly show you and your spouse how you can best leverage your time, resources, and skills for God's kingdom.

I believe that if you take the principles in this book and apply them, that you will have a blessed marriage and a blessed ministry. I am grateful that you were able to read this book to the end, which lets me know that you are hungry for the things of God. Remember ministry was not designed to become a mistress, but it was designed to minister to God's people. Grace and peace be upon your marriage from this day forward, and even forevermore.

CPSIA information can be obtained at www.ICGtesting.com
Printed in the USA
BVOW07s0451160614

356427BV00001B/5/P